START

COLLEGE SMART®

START

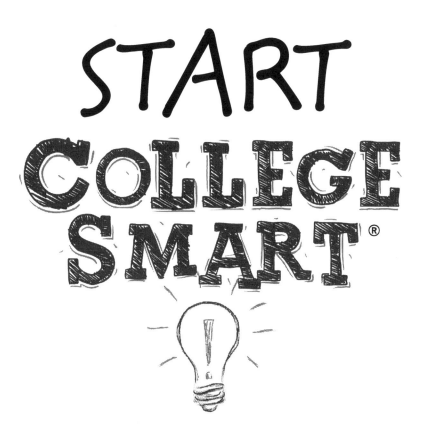

COLLEGE SMART®

For college & high school students on their way.
What to expect. How to succeed.
Find a career path.
And more. . ..

ROBERT R. NEUMAN, PhD

ISBN-13: 978-0-9961385-2-9

Editing: Jude Neuman
Design & Layout: AuthorsSupport.com

To Steve and Bill Harrison
Great minds think alike

To Baker Bill Bauske
Because learning is like a layer cake

Table of Contents

WHY IS COLLEGE IMPORTANT? WHAT SHOULD YOU GET FROM IT?

Have you been asked that question a lot? If not, ask yourself right now.

Most students choose these reasons:

1. Get a good job (the #1 reason)
2. Get a good education
3. Have a good time
4. Make new friends
5. Discover more about myself
6. All of the above

*I hope you chose "all of the above." College is an experience **of** a lifetime and **for** a lifetime. It's preparation for life and how you'll live it.*

Now if you think about what I just said, I mean *really think about it,* you're well on your way to understanding why college is important for you. There are a lot of ways that the importance of college goes over the heads of a lot of college students. I don't want that to happen to you.

1

I've given advice to more than 12,000 college students for more than 25 years. I've written a book about succeeding in college, called **CollegeSmart**. It's a good book. You should look at it.

Right now, I'm going to give you bits and pieces, chunks and barrels, of advice. **I want to get you started understanding everything you need to know.**

- Does that sound like I'm bragging? I am.
- Will I give you straight talk? I will. If you think that your college education is important, then we're on the same page.

College is not high school away from home! So what else is new? Well, you'd be surprised how many new college freshmen — and even older college students — think that they are moving from 12th grade in high school to 13th grade when they start college. They couldn't be more mistaken.

LOOK INSIDE YOURSELF. LET'S TAKE STOCK...

High school should have prepared you for college, but maybe it didn't. How do you judge how really ready you are for college? Here are a few things to ask yourself. And if I'm going to help you, you have to be really honest. I'm being honest with you. You do the same with me. Okay?

How many hours did you study each week in high school? 5, 10, more? Colleges want you to study at least **25-30 hours as a freshman** — then increase that number year after year.

Okay, now did you say to yourself, *"In high school, when my homework was done, I quit."*

Let's get this straight right away. *Homework* is a grade-school concept. The teacher tells you to do an assignment at home. You do it. End of story. So leave any idea like that of homework or *studying as much as you need to* in the past.

If you're going to be a successful college student, a real college learner — who gets the most out of college and graduates on-time — **you must study a certain maximum of hours** (not minimum) each week. Every week. **That's one big thing that makes college different from high school.**

Here's an analogy I often use with students to explain this point.

Say you're an athlete or maybe a musician. In high school, you worked at being the best athlete or musician you could be. But how good were you when you *left* high school? Are you ready to play in the NCAA? Are you ready to play in the Chicago Symphony orchestra or a famous band?

3

College is the major leagues, a famous symphony orchestra, or a headlining band.

COLLEGE IS <u>NOT</u> 13TH GRADE. SO…

So you have to ask yourself, *"Am I ready for college? Do I have the ability that it takes to study? To do the work?"* If you don't know these answers, starting the first day of college, you'll really be lost.

Clue: **If you're one of the 66%** of college-bound high school seniors who studied fewer than 5 or 6 hours a week, you're not ready. So you'll have to adjust, and I'll tell you how.

Another number: Research reports that **40% of freshmen say they're "overwhelmed."** Now you know why. Here's a really significant wrinkle to this number: *They don't know why.* But now <u>you</u> do.

HOW ABOUT YOUR H.S. GRADES?
ARE THEY AN INDICATOR?

Was high school easy for you? Did you get high grades most of the time? Did you feel really challenged? Do you feel like you learned a lot and that you're carrying that knowledge with you to college?

That truth of the matter is —

- Most college freshmen don't know how much they were challenged in high school.
- They don't know if they remember high school knowledge. **A truth: If they crammed for tests, they don't. It's gone.** So they don't know if they're *really* ready to handle the same subject at the college level — or a brand-new subject, for that matter.

**ONLY 35% GRADUATE ON-TIME.
SOBERING, ISN'T IT?**

I'm giving you this statistic so you understand why developing a college attitude is so very important.

Don't assume that just being IN college makes you able to meet its academic challenges. Getting *into* college is one thing. *Graduating* is a very different story. The statistics back this up.

HOW YOU DEVELOP A COLLEGE ATTITUDE

You say to yourself:

- *"This is not high school. I can't be over-confident about getting high grades in all my courses. I can't expect this to be a walk in the park. It's work, more like climbing a mountain."*
- "Course after course, semester after semester, year after year, *I've got a lot to learn, so...*
    - ◊ *"I'll have to make room for study every day whenever I can."* Morning, noon, or night.
    - ◊ *"As much money as my family and I are paying for college, I need to get our money's worth."*
    - ◊ *"I want to get the most out of my college education."* Why? Because...
    - ◊ *"My college education should lead me to a career. I want to make sure that happens."*

The overwhelming majority of college students' #1 reason for going to college is to "get a better job and make more money."

Those students who start college with the wrong attitude — that they've *got it made because they did well in high school* — usually end up spending extra years in college. No one can afford that. What's more, they end up with a college record they wouldn't want a future employer to see. If you take my advice, this won't be you.

So let me ask you. Can you feel humble? And I don't mean timid, or shy, or meek — just the opposite.

- College takes muscle, mental muscle
- It takes power, willpower
- It takes strength of mind and body

You've got a job to do. So go to it! College is a big contest, and you want to emerge a big winner. But this outcome isn't automatic.

IT'S ALL UP TO YOU. MAKE IT OR BREAK IT.

In college, you can no longer rationalize why your grades are low. You can no longer use these excuses:

- *"I'm just not good in that subject."*
- *"That professor is just boring. I can't stay awake in class."*
- *"The test wasn't fair. It was too tough."*
- *"My courses this semester are really hard."*
- *"I didn't know those things were going to be on the test."*
- *"The course moves so fast. I can't keep up."*
- *"I just don't have enough time to study."*

If you try to use these excuses with a college professor, you're just going to get a blank stare. **In college, you're accountable.**

Unlike other levels of education, you don't automatically graduate in a set number of years. You don't have to graduate at all.

In high school, did you try to "squeeze your study time in" around your personal time? In college, it's just the opposite. **To succeed, you nail down your study time first. Then schedule your social time around it.**

YOUR FUTURE: CAN YOU SEE IT YET?

Have you asked yourself about anything or everything that will come after college? What do you see for yourself after college? More education? A job, a career, a profession?

Be a student who asks questions. College is the time to ask all kinds of big questions and look for honest answers. Don't avoid these questions because they're big, hard, and take time to answer. You need these answers now. Whether or not you realize it, **you're just a few steps away from the rest of your life. College is THE time and place to....**

- Ask the big questions about yourself, your life, your goals, and your hopes.
- Find out who you are as a person. It's called self-knowledge. Strengths? Weaknesses? Capabilities? Talents? Things you need to work on?
- To leave behind any naïve ideas you have about what it takes to learn.
- To make learning as important as breathing.

Am I exaggerating? Nope. Take all these things to heart. Right now, you may not think they're important. But they are. Keep reading, and I'll convince you. Honest.

DO YOU KNOW HOW TO LEARN? YOU MIGHT BE SURPRISED.

How do you learn? This isn't a biological question. I'm asking this question at a very basic level. How do you learn? Again, **believe it or not, a lot of students didn't know the answer before they got to college.**

You can't learn without studying. Some students say they learn everyday by just being awake and walking around. That's true. But consider this. If you eat at a Chinese restaurant, how much have you learned about China? Well, you learned about Chinese dishes and that a good many are prepared in a wok. You have learned *something*.

But if you take a course in college about the History of China, knowing about egg foo young won't get you very far. You have to learn geography, history, traditions, politics, art, and so forth. Now you're beginning to learn. That takes work. Learning takes effort. Maybe you know this. Maybe not.

Another example? You take a vacation to the Grand Canyon. You can wonder at its size. Maybe you take a tour on horses. Maybe you watch a few programs at a visitor's pavilion. What you learn can be fascinating and interesting. But how much have you learned about geology or ecology or many other "ologies"? If you find you really like these ologies, you have to study, maybe there's a future in it for you!

That's "walking around" knowledge and it's important. The last thing you want is to walk around in a daze, noticing nothing. However, "walking-around knowledge" is not the kind of knowledge you're expected to gain as a college student.

- In college, you can't learn just by going to class and *sitting there*. You have to be active and alert.
- You can't learn by hanging around campus. There's no osmosis at work to infiltrate your system.
- You learn at the last-minute before a test. Cramming won't work and it isn't learning. It's memorizing for a few hours.
- You can't learn by knocking out a haphazard paper the night before it's due. That's panic, not learning.

LEARNING ISN'T PASSIVE OR RUSHED. IT'S ACTIVE AND REGULAR.

STUDYING. What a concept!

The only way you really learn something, completely and permanently — the way college professors expect — is to STUDY, STUDY, STUDY. This brings us around to what I said earlier. In college you're expected to study to the max. **What does the mean?**

You have to set aside a certain amount of time to study each day, each week.

You have to study in a place that's right for learning. Not in front of a TV or around constant texting interruptions. Not with friends around or noise in the background; Not lying on your bed with your face in a pillow, *etc.*

I'll be saying a lot more about learning, studying, and developing your brain power later. For now, I think you get my message. Are you with me? Let's go. Stick with me on this next part. These ideas may be brand new to you.

I want you to really develop the right college attitude. I want you to use what I say and apply it every day in college. And guess what? Once you learn these concepts, skills, and attitudes, **you'll use them in the workplace and for the rest of your life!**

HOW LEARNING "WORKS" AND HELPS YOU WIN IN LIFE

Why do all of us have to go to school in the first place? From kindergarten, maybe even pre-school, through college and beyond. What's it all about? Read these two main reasons: why you want to be a learner/ a student — as well and as long as you can be.

REASON #1: TO LEARN ABOUT YOURSELF, THE WORLD, HOW LIFE WORKS, AND HOW YOU FIT IN.

This is the BIG PICTURE — of you. You learn about yourself: your talents and strengths, your shortfalls, what's difficult for you, how to strengthen your weaknesses. How to grab onto knowledge. How to keep it. How to use what you've learned for the good. How to solve problems. Be creative. Be responsible. Use initiative. Take action. Think well and make good decisions. *(Keep going....)*

Become more mature and learn the many ways you can grow. Become a member of the world. What's the world like? What goes on outside your very small circle of the world? Outside the US? Out in space? *(Keep going...)*

By being in school. Studying. Listening to your professors. Enlarging your understanding of life and the world. Forming views and values. Learning how to arrive at them by weighing options, not just following

13

the crowds. Developing a code of ethics. How to live each day according to that code. *(Keep going... you're almost there...)*

Reading and writing. Talking and listening. What are the issues? How can you make thing better? In short, you're learning to come out of yourself and discover your place in the world. You're learning *to be a human being that walks the planet.*

In brief, *you're becoming a person.* Later on, you'll use ALL of these many things and more to live the best life you can: in a career, in a family, as a person, both inside and out.

REASON #2: TO LEARN HOW TO LEARN. IT'S A LIFE SKILL YOU NEED.

What does that mean? School is far more relevant than you ever imagined. If you do it right, it will teach you how to learn — a fundamental skill for survival in so many ways. Granted we're no longer in caves. But the cave people who were smart and learned about their environment are the ones who survived. Take a lesson from that. And you, too, will be able to adapt to change, survive and prosper.

Take Math, for instance

What have you studied? Algebra, geometry, maybe even calculus. In those courses, you've learned how to "learn" mathematically. It's a life skill. I once used calculus to figure out whether or not a table in a furniture store would fit in our kitchen. What else?

Now you can —

- Do your taxes.
- Interpret statistics and charts.
- Budget your money; plan financially for your future.
- Know when it's the best time to borrow money to finance a house.

Because you know how to think mathematically, you can *really* control your life and make good decisions. Your life becomes easier because you can think mathematically — whether you're looking for a good deal on electronics, deciding which car gives you best value, or investing in the stock market.

Your knowledge of math is necessary. It also adds more fun and excitement — want to figure out the odds of winning a lottery? And it gives you confidence in making all kinds of decisions about how to handle and make sense of this part of your life.

Take History. This one may surprise you.

You learn about what's happened in the past: the American Revolution, when it happened and why (what caused it). In the process, you're also learning **1)** *how to learn history as a subject and retain it, and* **2)** *how to use it practically, every day.* **Number 2 helps you throughout your life.** *How?*

Imagine yourself in a job. You've been given the task of deciding about how to grow the sales of a soft drink. How do you do that?

1. Well, first, you have to see what's happened in the past. You look into the product's history: what's worked and what's failed. When have sales risen? Fallen? You analyze what may have caused sales to rise and fall. You need to pinpoint causes to learn from them.
2. Then you have to look at what the company is doing in the present. How are sales now? What's causing them to behave in that way?
3. Your job is to change the present to get to where you want to be in the future.

History is all about analyzing causes and effects. You're learning to segment actions, identify mistakes and understand eventual solutions. You're "dissecting" to understand. It's what you're doing with the soft drink sales. That's how you succeed.

In short, if you learn about historical events as a student, you've learned HOW to learn about the past and its importance right now: in the present, as you move into your future. And that applies to your personal life in the career you may choose. For example, in life, understanding the mistakes you made in the past — either personally or professionally — you're less likely to repeat them in the present and the future. It all started with learning history.

Yes, Foreign Language, too. Just to show you I'm serious

You not only learn about a second language, but <u>how</u> to memorize different terminologies and new technical languages associated with all kinds of fields — computer technology, medical research, marketing terms, even personal communication technology. All change and grow daily.

English. Think of it as communication. After all, we live in the Information Age.

You'll always be reading, interpreting, and *writing about/learning about* new "stuff" that can be used in your job or your future. Where did that all begin? In English courses. There you learned HOW to read closely, interpret what you read, and communicate clearly. Then build a case for your point of view (like how to grow sales of a soft drink).

You're a college student so you can get ready for life.

You can go down the whole list of subjects that you've studied and will study. They all teach you—

1. That the ability to learn is as important as what you learn.

2. To improve your mind, your intellect, your brain, and your resourcefulness.

3. To launch yourself successfully and confidently into your life after college.

LIFE IN THE 21ST CENTURY —
Fast-paced, reacting and changing — the constant need to improve

Throughout your life, you will always be learning, you'll always be a student. If you're not a skillful questioner and analyst who wants to gain new knowledge every day, you'll find yourself stuck in one place or another, never able to move ahead, never able to succeed.

Can you keep up?

The 21st century, your century, is already defined as a time of incredible and constant change. You've studied about the famous, or infamous, Industrial Revolution when, to put it too simply, people moved from the farms to the factory. How long did that take? Decades.

In your lifetime, the pace from the old ("farm") to the new ("factory") *occurs practically daily*. Want an example?

I often tell students to remember their first cell phone and then look at their Smartphone. It became a pocket computer in just a few years.

You can use this symbol of what your life as a professional or a career person will be. Change, change, change. Rapid change. Can you keep up with it? Yes, if you take your college education very seriously and study your brains out. **Learners are the people who will own the future: thinkers, analysts, innovators, and problem-solvers.** The U.S. competes globally these days.

- Learning in college is just like keeping up with modern society. You have to learn stuff constantly every day.
- You have to continually develop new learning skills — even as you retain and sharpen your old ones.
- Why? You guessed it. **Because you're going to be a student for the rest of your life. So you need to get good at it.**
- That idea should be exciting rather than frightening.

WHAT DID YOU JUST LEARN?

Don't miss this quick post-game analysis about being a student, a learner, a studier, a person who wants to expand and develop your mind.

1. Learning — deep and permanent learning — requires studying.

- Studying requires time.
- As you learn, you're learning not only about subjects, but how to learn. That's good. Why?
- Because you'll have to be a learner throughout your life. Think of it as a life skill. (I know I just said this. I want you to remember it.)
- College is the place, **and perhaps your last real chance**, to develop your mind, brain, and intellect to move on successfully and confidently after you graduate.

Physiologically, your brain is at its peak during your college years. Don't waste the power. Use it or lose it.

Throughout this book, I will always come back to main points and show the relationships between and among them. I will repeat things. That's important. Repetition is one of the many aspects of learning.

I'm now making what seems to be a big jump, but it's not. I'm going to move from advice about *how* and *why* to think about college. We're going to talk about the chances of your finishing a degree.

FINISHING COLLEGE: BE WARNED

Well, you might say, "*If I'm going to start college, I'm going to finish it.*" **That's what 84% of freshmen think.** *That's just the attitude you should have. It shows purpose and determination.* However, words have to be backed by actions.

I want to give you some very important — even essential — cautions, to keep in mind. I'll give them to you, first, in the form of the **stark statistics**.

- Only **1 out of 3 students graduate** from college **in the normal four years.** Caution: It never occurs to the other 60+% that they won't graduate on-time.
- By the time **six years have passed, only 60% of a class** will have graduated. Many of these students had the casual attitude, of "*I got into college — that means I'll finish it.*" That's wrong.
- Do the math. How many students still have not earned a degree by the 7th year? **Nearly 40%.**

Now, some people will argue that college just takes longer for some students than for others. That may be true for a few; but not this many. *What's wrong?*

1. **Many, many students are not prepared for college work** because they don't know that college demands much more time and effort than high school. Always keep in mind what I said earlier: college is NOT just the next level above high school. It's a very large step.

2. **Far too many students arrive at college without any sense of why they're really there — and what they intend to do after college.** They don't know what kind of degree they want. They don't know what to major in. Some high school — and even college — advisers have told them that they'll *eventually* discover an academic direction. *When is eventually?*

For these advisers, I have this question: "*Are you going to pay for the extra years in college for those students?*" For a small minority of students, majors will come to them — sort of like the story we told about a visitor to the Grand Canyon being drawn to geology. But most students have to *find* a major.

GOT A MAJOR? A PLAN? A DIRECTION? THE DETERMINATION TO SHAPE YOUR FUTURE?

If you haven't settled on a major or degree when starting college, that doesn't mean all is lost. Not at all. It's just that in your first year you have to do a lot of thinking about your academic direction. You have to ask a lot of people for advice. That's a big job. But you can't put it off. You can't say, "*Later is fine.*"

DON'T HAVE A MAJOR? WANT TO PAY 25-50% MORE FOR COLLEGE? NO? THEN TIME TO START THINKING...

College is really, really expensive. If you don't know what it's going to cost, ask your parents. **If you're in a private school, the cost is right up there with buying a house.**

> **In fact, think about it like this.** Pretend you're buying a house, the house of your dreams. You settle on a price. But then, suddenly, after you've lived in the house for a year, you're told that you have to pay 25% more, or 50% more. Can families afford that? Is it fair? That's what suddenly happens to 60+% of families with college students.

It's the Big Switch. You and your parents settled on a college you like and can afford. You've worked out all the finances. Then, after a couple of years, you discover you have to spend or borrow even more money than you originally planned to. For a number of reasons, that's what happens to families whose students delay choosing a major. Once these students finally decide on a major, they typically have to add more courses to fulfill the requirements of that newfound major.

Right now (and the subject is in the news all the time), students who graduated from college are **overwhelmed with debt.** They may be paying off that debt for who knows how many years. It's not a good way to launch a life.

THAT'S NOT GOING TO BE YOU. WHY?

When you start college, you're going to dive in and swim, not sink and take 6 years to graduate.

- If you have to work harder because you need to come up to college standards for studying and learning, you're going to do it. You'll know how because I'm going to tell you how.
- If you have to spend extra hours each week talking to profs and advisers to find and settle on a major or degree, you're going to do it.

Think about this. **So far your education has been pushed at you.** You **_had_** to be in school. You had no choice. Because you were younger, you needed a lot of pushing, a lot of guidance – from teachers, advisers, and, of course, from your parents.

I'm sure you've already guessed what I'm going to say next...

COLLEGE: COMPLETELY DIFFERENT.
Initiative and willpower are the name of the game.

Do you have what it takes? Or are you looking for something that feels more like high school? Can you make good decisions when they're hard ones? For example, can you forgo a basketball game because you have too much work to do that night? (I didn't say "all," just "one" basketball game.)

- *Can you set the alarm and roll out to your 8:00 am class?*
- *Do you have the willpower to go to class instead of hanging out with your friends in the Union?*

Most profs don't take attendance. College students are supposed to be mature enough to show up for class. So *how does this connect to pushing yourself that we just talked about above?*

YOU DON'T *HAVE* TO BE IN COLLEGE.

There will be no pushing or shoving by teachers and advisers in college. You might get that from your parents. But how effective will they be if you're not living at home?

- If you need pushing, who will do it? That's right. YOU.
- Encouragement? YOU.
- Setting goals each and every day? YOU.
- Organizing your days? YOU.
- Studying every day like it's a *full-time job* because it is? YOU.
- Acting less like an adolescent high schooler and more like a young adult who is just a few short years from LIFE? YOU.

 Remember how much you always wanted to "grow up"?

Here it is. It's all yours. Right now, as you read what I have to say, I'm doing the pushing and the shoving. I'm a pushy guy at times. But I also hope that I'm encouraging you. **You can do this.**

True—

- You have to use your time outside of class well.
- You have to keep a lot of details in mind. What? Where? When?
- You have to keep a lot of balls (courses) in the air.
- You have to answer a lot of questions.
- And you have to work hard.

If you haven't thought about the place of education and learning in your life, now's the time to do it. It's not an exaggeration to **say that your life will change dramatically if you successfully complete your college education.** Why? Let's answer that question.

YOUR FUTURE IN DOLLARS AND CENTS

As expensive as college is, college is one of the best, if not **the** best, investments that you'll make in your life. Just from a dollars-and-cents point of view, a college education will gain you a lot more money in your lifetime than someone without a college degree will earn. How much more?

Right now, if you were to look at two people from your generation who have just retired from a lifetime of employment, one with and one without a degree, guess how much more the college grad will have made than the non-grad. **$1,000,000.**

 It's true: one million dollars. These are the government's projections.

In your lifetime, you will earn **at least twice as much** with your college degree as the person who doesn't have one. Are you beginning to see how important your college education is? Take advantage of it. Don't be halfhearted about it. If you had a cranky, no-nonsense uncle, he's say, *"Grow up and make it work!"* It's a life-altering gift, especially if your parents are footing the bill. Do you remember my comparison about the cave dwellers? Your uncle would understand it. He's lived longer than you. I'm glad I brought up the cave dwellers again because they adapted to change and were able to survive.

A DEGREE: HOW IT RELATES TO YOUR CAREER FLEXIBILITY

This college degree will enable you to —

- choose from a lot of different jobs
- move from one job to another within the workplace
- advance in your profession

- get more satisfaction out of your career
- even change professions altogether

In short, your college degree, your college education, will give you a lot more career flexibility. You'll worry less. You'll also feel a lot more confident if your employer throws you unexpected curve balls. Or if **we have a repeat of The Great Recession of 2008.** Here's a fact of employment life you have to keep in mind.

In the 21ˢᵗ century, your century, changes in work and jobs and careers will happen in an instant. Success belongs to innovators, thinkers, and problems-solvers. (Yes, I'm repeating myself.)

Important point: Repetition is a key to learning!

Do you recall what I said earlier about cell phones as opposed to your mobile devices? Even that simple change can alter how people work. They're always "reachable." Think about the monumental changes brought on by the whole newly-computerized world you live in and will continue to live in. What do you think that does to the speed of work?

Living in a changing world, you have to be ready. How do you do that? You're right again. **You adapt.** How? By being an adept learner with a college education behind you in the workplace.

- With your college degree, you'll be able **to succeed when you return to "school" as your job requires.** Whether it's online education, back to a traditional classroom, going to seminars or programs that your career demands, you have to be intellectually ready to learn.
- You'll be **learning new technologies and ways of doing things every day** on the job: you must be able to stay on top of things in your profession or work world.
- What if you want to **continue your education right after college? Or in a few years?** Let's say you want or need to go to graduate school to pursue your career dream. What if you want to be an

orthodontist, a tax specialist? a psychologist? What if you're in business, and you need an MBA to advance? For all these things, you'll need an impressive college record to continue your education. You'll need high grades from beginning to end. **And you'll need test-taking skills to successfully score on the qualifying tests that all professional schools demand.**

 I mentioned earlier that you have to make your whole college experience work because you're the one at the "controls."

BE THE CAPTAIN OF YOUR SHIP. WATCH THE COMPASS.

What does a captain do to make sure the boat/ship doesn't end up on the rocks? Keep the craft in good working order and map out a well-planned route to each destination.

- As a college student, **that means refining and developing your learning skills** each day because they keep you moving in the right direction toward your goals — day to day and semester to semester.
- As captain, you must be organized and follow a predetermined course and timetable. How does that translate to you as a college student? It means you have to have a Daily/Weekly **Map. Follow it. Stay the course on reaching your goals. You may also discover smaller, bountiful ports along the way.**

True. College will give you a class schedule. But what is the first thing you notice about that schedule? **You're scheduled to be in class perhaps less than half the time as high school.**

IT'S NOT FREE TIME.

Wow! With all those hours that you don't have to be in class, you can do whatever you want. Right? Wrong. Wrong. Wrong. If you waste all those "free" hours during the week, the result will inevitably be failure. Those hours are not free.

Why are you given that time? To study outside of class for about 30 or so hours a week.

Listen up. How many times have I mentioned that college study is a full-time job? I can't emphasize it enough. **Most learning in college takes place <u>outside</u> of class.**

How do you stay on a "studying track?" **You get organized. You create a Time Map. There's one on page 33. Use pencil when organizing your map. Let's do this thing! Right now. Grab a pencil.**

1st Fill in the times you are in class.

2nd Then, plug in blocks of time for study. Do they add up to 25-30 hours? If not, rework them. That's why you have the pencil.

3rd **THEN** you add personal time, social time with friends, clubs, or activities. But schedule them, too. Note: They have a begin time and an end time. Don't go out with the gang for pizza for a couple hours after an activity.

4th Do it right, and your **Map** shows what you should be doing every hour of every day, even how you're using your *truly* free time.

5th Don't forget sleep time. Get enough of that, too, or nothing goes right. Research repeatedly proves it — even if you don't think it's hurting you. It is. In ways you don't understand. Don't hang out with the dorm crew until the wee hours. **Research shows that students who get only 6-6.5 hours of sleep will drop by one letter grade. They can't think.** They also develop serious medical problems. Define your sleep time, and stick to it.

 MOST students get only 6-6.5 hours of sleep.

Everything gets entered into your **Map.** That's how you know your week is do-able. If there's too much, what should you eliminate? There are only so many hours in a week. Time is finite. (Again, that's why you're using a pencil, so you can erase and make changes until the **Map** works.) In the future, you can use a digital calendar, but right now we're doing this together.

Post copies of your **Map** on your computer, on your desk, in notebooks, everywhere, even your bathroom mirror. It keeps you on track. Keep it in front of you at all times.

Stay with me on this. It's fundamental to your success. I know I've been pitching and tossing lots of things at you so far. (There's a lot more to come; but we'll get through it. Have confidence.)

	Sun	Mon	Tue	Wed	Thu	Fri	Sat
7:00							
8:00							
9:00							
10:00							
11:00							
12:00							
1:00							
2:00							
3:00							
4:00							
5:00							
6:00							
7:00							
8:00							
9:00							
10:00							
11:00							
Total							

GETTING IT TOGETHER. ORGANIZATION IS EVERYTHING!

*F*ollow your **Time Map**: carefully, precisely, every day. It's the only way to get it all done, and do it well, *including rest and relaxation*. I know it sounds funny to plan for R & R. But it's important that you build it in. Here are two more items you have to build into your **Map**.

- Time for talking to people who might help you find a major that will make you happy and fulfilled. If they don't know, they can refer you to someone more helpful. Getting started is the important thing.
- Time you'll need to bring your studying and learning skills up to college level.

Think of all the time you need to set *not only daily goals*, like keeping up in all your courses and getting that big paper done, *but long-term goals,* like what you want to do after college, for the rest of your life.

It's easier to make a Time Map than follow one. That takes will-power and focus. Earlier I compared being a learner to being an athlete or musician who wants to get better and better. Competing at a higher and higher athletic level takes developing your body and increasing your knowledge of your particular sport. As a musician, you won't be able to play more advanced music unless you daily develop your playing skills. So it is with learning.

> **Your college courses will no doubt be a lot harder (and should be) than high school. They cover twice the material in half the time.**
>
> Plus, what you're learning is more difficult.
>
> **Content remembered for life.** Not only do you have to learn faster, you have to learn more deeply, more thoroughly, and then retain that knowledge permanently, not just from test to test. That takes time.

Here's the plan: study is a full-time job → find the time → create the map → follow it → get your money's worth.

And here we are back to my original points. College studying has to be a full-time job. One of the first requirements of a full-time job is showing up for work (going to class), then managing their time to get all the work done: hour-by-hour, day-by-day. Why do you have to be so careful with your time? To —

1. gain knowledge
2. get your money's worth on your college investment
3. develop sharp learning skills that you'll need throughout your life.

BEWARE THE BIG TALKER WHO THROWS TUITION AWAY

A student might tell you, *"Oh. That class is easy. I hardly studied at all and still got a high grade."* This statement violates all three goals above.

1. This student worked for the grade, not the knowledge (goal #1).
2. Also, how can any college student — in good conscience — have that outlook when college is so expensive? This consumer didn't get his/her money's worth (goal #2) from that course.

Let's talk dollars for a moment: **What does a year cost in college?**

Currently, at a private college, about $30,000; at a state school, $9,000; and for an out-of-state student in a state school, $22,000. Now multiply by 4 for the cost of four years. **You owe it to yourself and your family to learn.**

Here's another interesting way to look at your education. Use the numbers above to calculate how much you pay for each class. Are you sure you want to cut your 8:00 a.m. Bio class?

3. Students who don't study and still *get a good grade* feels like they got away with something. In truth, they cheated themselves by not "flexing" their learning skills (goal #3). I would ask about that grade in more detail. A few profs have a reputation as "easy graders" but they're an extremely rare breed.

You shouldn't care how "easy" a course may be or how the professor grades. You're doing this for yourself, not the prof. You still should give that course its share of your study time *because you're paying for it, and because there is always more to learn in any subject.*

This is your education. Make it meaningful. You're the one who's going to make sure that when you leave college, you've gained as much as you could — not as little as you were able.

COURSES AND CLASSROOMS.

Y*ou have your course schedule and **Personal Map**, you've built in 30 hours to study, and you're ready for the semester to begin.*

THE FIRST TWO WEEKS

Whenever a semester begins, recite this: **"The first two weeks are the most important weeks of the semester."** Why? Think about it this way.

Imagine yourself as an athlete starting a very important game. As soon as it starts, you don't just stand around waiting for the other side to score. Obviously not. You charge ahead applying all the strength and skill you've developed to win.

Your courses are like athletic contests: You plan and play to win. From the very first day of class, you're going to plan for success. Some examples of things you should do:

1. **Familiarize yourself with what's coming.** Even before you enter the classroom, look over all of your textbooks and any other materials you've had to buy for your courses. Page through them from beginning to end to see what they're like. Then read the first chapter or section. See, you're already ahead of the game.

2. **Find a good seat,** maybe not in the front row, but certainly not in the back. Sit where it's easy to pay attention. Lessen distractions.

3. **Unplug.** Before class starts, you turn off your phone. Your professor will probably tell you to anyway. And take my word for it, because I've taught many college courses, there's no better way to get yourself on the professor's dummies list than have your device go off or to be seen texting, *etc.*

4. **Pay attention when the professor goes through the course outline.** In college, it's called a *syllabus*. It will probably contain an overview of everything that will be covered in the course.

   - What the course "rules" are for things like phones, or using your laptop
   - What happens when you miss a deadline
   - The grading policy
   - The number of grade-able items in the course
   - Other details you should know about the course

5. **Keep your course calendar safe.** It will include —

   - due-dates for assignments
   - when tests will occur
   - what to read before each class to be ready for the class discussion.

6. **Hang on to the syllabus. It will define how your final grade will be calculated.**

   - You'll see how many exams you have, as well as quizzes or written assignments.
   - You'll also see how much each test, assignment and quiz "counts." Pay close attention to this information because your life in the course depends on it.

It's not helpful to get an A on a quiz that counts 10% and a C on a midterm that counts 30%.

7. **Know this: You'll be tested on <u>all</u> material** from the course: text books and class notes. **Even things you never talked about in class.** There's only so much class time; some things won't be discussed in class. They're fair game on a test because the information was assigned as reading.

ABOUT TESTS AND GRADING

Few tests. College courses have fewer exams, sometime as few as two or three. What does that mean? I'm sure you can guess. **If you blow even one test, you can blow your final grade.**

No do-overs. Also, in general, college professors don't do make-up tests or extra-credit assignments to offset a low exam grade. This is a big difference from high school: where you may have tests every week with many kinds of opportunities to make up any low grades.

About finals. Even though the syllabus may not mention it (it's just assumed you know it), **final exams are almost always cumulative.** The final may, and probably will, **cover everything** and anything from the first day of class. That's another big reason to stay on top of your courses from day one. Cramming can't cut it.

So whatever you do, don't imagine that college coursework is anything like high school.

HOW TO THINK ABOUT REGULAR STUDY

S *tudy according to your Time Map.* *It keeps you on track every day and every week. Unlike high school, you must study* *at least* *25 hours each week, or at least 2 hours for each credit you're taking in college.*

In other words, if you carry a 15-hour credit load, you should be studying a minimum of 30 hours per week. Does it take your breath away?

I want you to cast your mind back to the "good old days" in high school. If you were like most high school students, you didn't have to study very much at all outside of school. You might have had to "do your homework," but that probably didn't take much time or effort. Most high school students don't have to study beyond doing their homework to get high grades. Instead, they "cram."

 Newsflash! Cramming doesn't work in college. There's too much to cram.

"Homework" is really a grade-school concept. Teachers tell students to do assignments at home to **emphasize that learning occurs even after school**. That was a good thing for young students to understand. But when older students — in middle and high school — continued to think that learning was the result of only doing homework, their study and learning abilities got stuck in the mud. They're still operating at a grade school mentality.

IN COLLEGE, THERE'S VERY LITTLE HOMEWORK. BUT LOTS OF STUDY.

Let's straighten some things out. First, get rid of the concept of doing your homework. **That implies that you wait for your teachers to tell you what to do outside of class.** You won't succeed in college if you hold onto those simple beliefs.

The great majority of professors simply expect students to follow the course syllabus and study as much as necessary to master course material. It's your responsibility to do the job.

This is not to say that college professors will never ask students to complete certain short assignments to turn in the next day. But it's rare.

In other words, it's up to you to assign yourself homework, which, in college, means <u>studying</u> for each of your courses to keep up with the professor. Just eliminate the idea of *homework* from your vocabulary.

EFFICIENT LEARNING IS LIKE A LAYER CAKE.

For many years now, I've told college students to think about studying and learning as a birthday cake with lots of layers. It's my metaphor to show how learning occurs in layers.

Let me explain. I'm going to take you through the several steps (layers) that will make you the most effective studier and learner you can be. Let's take just one of your possible courses; for example, *Introduction to Psychology*.

You looked at the course syllabus, and you see that in the next class, your professor will introduce a new topic.

Layer 1: Read the assigned chapter **before** you go to class. **Take notes based on your reading** and enter them into your computer file for the course.

Layer 2: Go to class (more about that later), and listen to the prof's presentation along with the questions of other students.

Here's the big benefit: Because you have completed the first layer, pre-reading and preparation, your prof is actually *reviewing* the chapter *for you* in class. Plus, any questions you ask will be particularly significant — they'll clarify or enlarge upon what you already sort of know.

You take notes in class — in a notebook or laptop, no matter.

Just taking the notes, writing down what is said in the class, helps you broaden your understanding of the subject. This is now your ***third pass on this topic***, and you're only in the first class presentation! You're way ahead of the game already.

Layer 3. Take your notes back to your room and review them by rewriting them (keying in your file or writing in your notebook by hand. See what works better for you).

You might ask, *"Isn't that just doing the same thing over and over?"* Yes! Repetition is fundamental to the learning process. With each repetition, your knowledge gets broader and deeper. And that's what you ultimately want to achieve.

So layers lead to a better understanding of everything in your course on a class-by-class basis. You're building your knowledge every day. You use the same routine for each class: pre-read, take notes, listen in class, take more notes that you don't have from your reading, ask questions to clarify, rewrite your notes after class.

If you don't study with this kind of tactic, you'll always be cramming at the last-minute for tests and pulling all-nighters to finish papers. And, even worse, forgetting what you've crammed — and earning low grades.

I understand that laying out the plan of action is a lot easier than doing it. After all, you're the one who has to follow the steps — applying them to all your courses and each class meeting. However, it becomes a comfortable routine and keeps you at the top of your game.

At the heart of this plan is, of course, being faithful to your daily and weekly Map. But as you follow the schedule and apply the layers of studying, you will get better and better at both.

Want to play guitar in a rock band that gets gigs and earns money? If you think you might qualify for such a band, you've probably been taking music lessons for awhile. You might even write music. How did you get so good? You practiced, practiced, and practiced.

How do you get really good at learning?

- You know the first part: You study, study, study.
- Now you're learning that your best results will come from studying with a method – studying in layers. After every course and semester, you can give yourself a big party, complete with candles of your *brilliance* glowing on top of the cake. Treat yourself. Celebrate your layering technique.

FIND A QUIET PLACE

I n high school, when you studied, where did you study? At the kitchen table? In your room with the TV on one side of the room and a computer game going on the other? How about in the gym at half time?

I'm exaggerating to make a point. I'm sure you know what's coming. In college, you have to study in a place where you can concentrate and focus on the work in front of you. So along with shaking off all those other bad habits from high school, you have to do the same regarding study location.

Dorms are often like shopping malls with people coming and going, in and out of stores (rooms), making noise, *etc.* So if you really want to study in your room, it takes planning and dedication to get it done. You might have to coordinate times with your roommate. But even if you create a threatening *Do Not Disturb Sign* for your door to keep the invaders out, you'll still have the din in the hallways.

Most likely, you'll have to escape the turmoil of a residence hall to do your best studying. Find a quiet place. **You'll study more productively, and it will take less time to do so**. Where do you go? Many colleges have designated study areas where students are expected to be quiet out of respect to students trying to concentrate. Sometimes it works. Often, it doesn't. Study lounges can become social gathering places.

You might have to get creative to find a quiet place.

A study area can be any big room with tables and chairs. How about an empty dining hall? There may be empty meeting rooms otherwise used by clubs and societies.

Student Unions have places that may be marked off for studiers. They're places you have to find, but the search is worth it. Usually these kinds of places are populated by serious studiers who show up regularly but respect each others' quiet time. No one bothers anybody. No one entertains visitors. These are real study places.

Of course, **libraries** are often great places to study. Most students in libraries usually work silently, so anyone can work there in peace and quiet. If you're lucky, you may get a closed-door carrel. A carrel is an individual closed-off space for quiet study, usually found in the stacks of a library.

Whether you find one favorite comfortable place to study or several, make sure you study in privacy, solitude. Ideal places are generally out of the way of student traffic and irritating noise and distractions.

I promise that if you find good places to study, you will study better and more efficiently. You'll get more done in less time! And have more personal time!

Look at the big picture again – the big WHYS and HOWS and WHATS.

Are you getting a deeper insight into why you personally think college is important for you?

Are you developing confidence that you *can* accomplish the goal of higher education? (Always keep in mind that *it is higher.*)

Do you have a better handle on what it is that you want to accomplish with a successful college degree as you take it into your future?

I'll keep on bringing up these important questions again and again. I want them to really sink into your head so that you have no choice but to design good answers for yourself.

This is all about you, after all — your life, your learning strength, your sense of purpose.

YOUR APPROACH TO COURSES: Pro-active and positive.

T ake courage. Be confident. You can do this. Enlarge your comfort zone. You won't believe what you can do if you take the first steps. You'll find out it's a whole lot easier than you thought. It's the beginning of developing leadership traits. The world is waiting for you.

YOUR RELATIONSHIPS WITH PROFS— THEY'RE YOUR COACHES.

In high school, you sat in the same classes every day. The classes were relatively small, so you got to know your teachers.

Now you should get to know your profs: despite fewer classes a week, despite far more students in a class, and despite that your professor may seem remote or distant at times.

Don't be put off. The thing you can always count on with college professors: They are experts in their particular academic area — they like to demonstrate that in the classroom. And, if you go see them during their office hours, they will love talking to you about their subject.

When professors hold office hours without students, it's unbelievably boring. Since you're now a student who always has questions (because you want to know more and get your money's worth), you'll want to get to know your profs.

Go ask them questions. Clarify things said in class. Make connections: Go talk to your Econ prof about what you're learning about the Industrial Revolution in History class.

Have a problem with the course? Visit the professor during office hours. Don't delay. Remember how fast college courses move? Iron out the problem while it's still fixable. Remember: One concept builds on another. Wait too long to go for help, and you're sunk.

ABOUT "BOREDOM." IT DISAPPEARS IF YOU GET OFF THE BENCH AND GET IN THE GAME.

Oh, how often I've heard this complaint from students — usually as an excuse for getting low grades:

- The professor is boring
- The course is boring
- With all this boredom, the student just can't get excited to learn or motivated to succeed.

Actually, boredom occurs, not for the reasons above, but more often, **because it's the result of how disinterested or tired the student may be.** You can't expect professors to act like Chris Rock in the classroom or some animated computer character.

Remember what I said earlier about the difference between high school teachers and college professors? Most high school teachers still push you to succeed, if only minimally, to help you keep your education on track from year to year.

However, **college professors are not going to push you or sweet-talk you, or persuade you to like them, the subject, or the course**. It is laid out for you as a big challenge to your intellect. You are expected to be accountable for your learning. Totally. You're on your own.

YOU HAVE TO SUIT UP FOR EVERY COURSE.

It's part of growing up. You don't have to like everything about your courses, but you do have to respect them.

You're the one in charge of everything. Your success depends mainly on your effort and determination to succeed. To go back to the athletic image, **the ball is in your court. Do something with it.**

Repetition is the way you learn and remember the material. I know I'm repeating myself. It's intentional. See the recap below.

WHAT HAVE YOU LEARNED ABOUT WORKING IN COLLEGE COURSES?

One more time: College is not high school. It's not the 13th grade. To review, here are the differences:

- The large amount of knowledge you have to master
- The speed at which you must master it
- The high performance your professors expect
- The way grades are strictly calculated
- As captain of your ship, you stay your course. Don't let students who don't care about their courses influence your attitude. Don't hang out with negative students who complain and find fault all the time.
- You're going to stay on top of all your courses by following your **Map**, going to every class, keeping up with readings and class notes, never waiting until the last-minute to prepare for tests and class assignments.
- Each day, from class to class, you'll get more and more involved in all your courses:
  ◊   to master them.

◊   to learn for the long term (beyond your final exam, beyond the semester, and beyond graduation).

- From day to day, you stay focused on understanding your direction and goals throughout college — and beyond.

So to return to my athletic comparison. With every one of your college courses, you have to know the rules of the game. You have to talk to your coach. You have to know what kind of challenges you will face to earn a high final grade *and get the most out of every course* — semester after semester.

I know. I know. I sound like a sports coach, right? Pretend I'm blowing a whistle. Let's do this!

You go to college for many reasons, but these are the main reasons, upon which all the others are built:

1. By taking college courses, **you develop study methods that become part of you.** In other words, they become a permanent way that you think and learn.

2. Real learning — specifically, long-term learning — comes from **systematic and effective study** methods and **regular habits** that you apply to your courses daily.

3. Finally, when you learn, two things should happen:

   a.) You should **gain knowledge** — the specific material, matter, or "stuff" that your professors expect you to learn in all your courses;

   b.) You should **develop an all-embracing learning ability** that you can apply to anything you have to learn in the future.

It's as simple as it is important. Throughout your life, you will have to attain new knowledge every day — personally as well as professionally. And because significant knowledge does not simply happen by glancing at it, you have to study it so it sticks in your brain — permanently.

Here's a daily motto for you. Post it on the mirror above your sink, and stare at it as you brush your teeth.

Studying leads to learning.

When you learn, you gain knowledge.

You also develop the ability to learn, a skill you'll need constantly in your future.

The future may refer to your classes next semester; or when you graduate and start a career; or when you want to advance in your profession; or even change careers.

ABOUT CHEATING

I t exists, and so many students don't understand that "It's still wrong, even if you don't get caught." I'm talking about doing things like —

- *copying exam answers*
- *using a friend's work as your own*
- *lying to your professor about missing a test or a deadline*
- *plagiarism*

Let's talk about plagiarism: buying the work/writing of someone else — commonly from the Internet — and submitting it as your own work. Judging from my own general research on the Internet, students in high school frequently plagiarize. They get a topic from their teacher to write about. They go to the Internet to find something someone else has written. Then they turn in that work as their own. Or they simply buy a paper.

I don't know a better way of making my point other than to say, DON'T DO IT. IT COULD DESTROY YOUR WHOLE COLLEGE CAREER.

Colleges treat all matters of cheating like robbery. And that's exactly what it is. Plagiarism is stealing from someone else: using another person's thoughts, ideas, and words.

Now some students may treat my warning like the one that appears at the beginning of movies. You know, the one that essentially says, *"If you copy this movie, you are subject to fines and even jail time."*

However, a college is not a movie audience of millions. Colleges are smaller communities — no matter how large their enrollment — that are always trying to maintain the integrity of the community. When you're in a place where the honesty of researchers and scholars is paramount, cheating students are intolerable, and faculty have no mercy when they discover plagiarism. **And they do have their ways.**

You know, as a dean, I often had to chair Disciplinary Committees to judge cheating cases, usually plagiarism. When a case was proven, a student would be penalized with an *F* in the course. If the misconduct was very serious, like plagiarizing a term paper that counted for most of a student's final grade, the student might be asked to leave the college for at least one semester.

Many professors will state in their course syllabuses the standard of honesty in their course — plus any ensuing penalties for dishonesty.

I recommend that you read about plagiarism on the Internet. You'll find there, for example, regulations concerning plagiarism at different universities. Read them; understand them; take them to heart. Please. Not only is cheating unethical. It's very risky, **too risky to chance it.**

I've personally seen what happens to students in the aftermath of a cheating conviction. It's like being convicted of a crime. You may not go to jail, but **wrongdoing can follow a person even beyond college**. Do your own work.

BEING ABLE TO COMMUNICATE.
A major power in your life.

Let's talk about communication: your special communication skills; the importance of communicating well in all circumstances; and the significance of being a good communicator in college and career.

What communication talent and expertise do you need to develop and sharpen?

- *writing*
- *reading*
- *talking*
- *listening*

When you were in high school, how did you rank yourself on each of these four types of communication? Were you a pretty good reader, but not so good at writing assignments, especially long ones? Did you groan a lot? Did you like talking to your friends, but not talking in class? Did you find it hard concentrating on what your teacher was saying — occasionally, frequently, or practically all the time?

Self-evaluate your ability at communication. Look backward to high school. It will help you see the present and help you look forward. That's what I want you to do, first from the point of view of your everyday life in high school.

- Besides school assignments, did you read other things for interest or enjoyment, or prefer not to?
- Maybe Harry Potter was just not your thing, but you did have a computer game passion. Did you read a lot about it?
- Did you like to read about cars, snowboarding, fashion, Hollywood stars?
- Did you watch a lot of movies, remembering every image on the screen and each word spoken by every character? Then did you discuss the movie with friends?
- What about in school? What kind of communication did you want to avoid or always try to?
- Maybe you didn't like reading long novels or, even worse, Shakespeare.
- When your math teacher called for answers from the class, did you hide behind the biggest person in the room, like your friend, the center on the football team?
- When you had to give an oral presentation in class, did you find yourself barfing in the john beforehand so that when you finally got in front of the class, the blood had all settled in your legs?
- When one of your teachers wanted to talk to you after class, did you find that you sounded as though you had lost your native language?

Let's jump from being in high school to being in your first big job. Here's your opportunity to start your professional life in a career you have dreamed about. You've planned and worked for it since you were a young college student, maybe even earlier.

Besides having the intelligence, knowledge, expertise, creativity, enthusiasm, and determination to do the job, what else will your bosses, managers, and coworkers expect of you? That you have excellent communication skills, equal to all those other qualities you bring to the job!

Can you imagine, even in your craziest daydreams, any job that does not require people to read, write, talk, and listen? And do it with intelligence, ease, style, and confidence?

Maybe they existed in the Agricultural Age or the Industrial Age, but certainly not in the Computer Age or Information Age.

Whether you become a mountain climber, a spy, a mad scientist, or an engineer, you'd better communicate well. You career may depend on it.

Let's jump back to college. Do we agree, then, that two of the most important aspects of college are 1) gaining knowledge and 2) developing learning skills? Yes! Now, let's add communication skills to the list of college biggies. Just about every job out there in the big wide world demands that your communication skills be competent. So, too, does every course you take in college.

Writing. Naturally, you will be asked to do more writing in your literature, history, and social science courses than in your natural and physical science courses. Usually, you wouldn't be asked to write a research paper in a math, engineering, or a computer science course, or give an oral presentation in your chem course.

However, considering all the courses you'll take in college — from your freshman to your senior year — you'll be expected to use all of the basic communication skills with proficiency. Whether you're composing lab reports or research papers, they must be at college-level in terms of grammar, spelling, sentence and paragraph structure, overall organization, and coherence.

Here's a headline from **The New York Times:** What Corporate America can't build? A simple sentence.

Right now, if you can write efficiently and clearly, you'll be valued by your employer. I've read —

- That more than 60% of emails are unclear, causing confusion and more work.

- That it takes most employees too long to write a simple memo. (Texting is generally frowned upon in business.)

- Fact: Most employees' writing skills **haven't developed since 9th grade.**

- That even executives come under fire because they cannot write understandably.

Looking for a way to distinguish yourself in the workplace? Become a great communicator.

Reading. Obviously, you have to read in all your courses in varying amounts. But whatever the courses, your reading has to be focused. You're going to have to read with concentration in the workplace.

Jump into the future once again. Few jobs do not require proficiency in reading and writing skills.

Now back to college. Consider talking and listening, the last two major communication skills. They're the ones that too many students either forget about or disregard as important. Everybody can talk, right? And if you talk with someone you have to listen, right?

There are two sorts of talking and listening. Let's refer to them as the formal and informal. I'm sure you know exactly what I mean.

When you use your communications informally, for example, you can be casual or relaxed. You may read quickly through a magazine or newspaper; you may write a short email to someone in your family; you chat when you're out for dinner or walking on campus with a classmate.

Different communication skills are needed in formal situations. Just look at what you do in college. Ask yourself these questions.

- How can I possibly know what's going on in a class without listening carefully or taking accurate notes?
- How can I understand what I'm supposed to learn without reading with concentration, highlighting select passages, and organizing good notes?
- How can I write an articulate and intelligent paper on what I've read, like a novel or some event in Econ, without knowing and applying all the basic rules of writing — from accurate spelling and grammar to coherent sentences, paragraphs, and a persuasive essay structure?
- When I ask questions in class or when I talk to my professor directly and privately (both of which you should do regularly), am I going to verbally stumble around and use a lot of *uhs* and *you knows* with lots of dead air space? Can I find words and assemble them intelligently? Or do I stammer and grope for words?

How can you make sure you don't make those mistakes? You make a special effort to develop your skills <u>anytime</u> you're reading, writing, talking, and listening.

By the way, when you are "listening," are you really paying attention to what the speaker is saying? Or are you thinking about what *you're* going to say next? Miscommunication leads to workplace mistakes.

TO RECAP:

Why? All together now: *"Because repetition helps you learn!"*

- College requires excellent communication skills both inside and outside of class.
- Along with gaining knowledge and learning how to learn better, you should be developing solid communication skills.
- You'll want to take these skills with you into your professional

world and your personal life later on. Just because you graduate is no guarantee that you're a good communicator. Graduating is not a magic wand. Becoming a good communicator takes ongoing practice.

What should happen when you're in school (at any level) in the classroom?

- You learn a particular subject, and what your teacher requires.
- You study the subject with concentration complete assignments well, and regularly prepare to take tests to prove you know your "stuff."
- You study thoroughly, so that you remember what you've learned.
- You look for relationships from one subject to another. Does one course tell you something about another? Don't compartmentalize your courses. Look for connections.
- Finally, you become creative and imaginative. Use everything you've learned from course to course and year to year wherever you can.

PARALLELS BETWEEN SCHOOL AND JOB YOU NEVER THOUGHT OF

First of all, you have a supervisor, manager, and boss. These are the people who make sure you have the knowledge to do your job. Your supervisor tells you how to use your school knowledge to help the organization, then assigns you work, and finally, evaluates your overall performance. That performance evaluation moves up the line and crosses the desks of your department manager, his/her boss, and so on.

That evaluation measures —

- how well you've done your job (or haven't)
- how much initiative you've brought to it
- how much you've advanced and improved yourself (striving to do better and learn more)
- how you have advanced the interests of your employer, by being a creative and imaginative problem-solver
- that you collaborate well with colleagues
- that you can be trusted to do your work — you're dedicated and dependable.

Does that sound like a combination of all the courses and teachers you've ever had? Doesn't this list describe what you're supposed to do in the classroom? Of course it does.

- Classrooms are like workplaces.
- You have a job to do that requires work on your part.
- You have assignments to finish.
- You have responsibilities to take care of.
- You're accountable to someone in charge.
- You have deadlines to meet.
- The quality of your work determines whether or not you move up the ladder.

Make a note of all that. Stick it on your desk or mirror, (getting crowded there, isn't it?). *Classrooms are practice for my career.* Don't downplay this really important concept. Other students may say —

"I just want to get through school and get a job" or

"Who needs to take this or that course?" or

"I don't have to go to that class because I can learn it on my own." (Do you think that going into work is optional? Not now it isn't.)

These kinds of students just doesn't get it. Whatever the course, even if they don't like it, even if it's hard, even if it doesn't seem relevant at the time, the course will add something to their ability later to do a great job.

Here's another one of my famous athletic analogies. Let's use a basketball player. If the only basketball you play is one-on-one in your driveway, even if you make a school team, I doubt that you'll play first string, if any string at all.

As you move from course to course and from one level of education to another, if you want to succeed, you have to progress from your driveway to the court. Then, as you advance from one team to the next, and the competition gets stronger, you'll gradually develop your talent, expertise, and confidence.

So let's go back to those questions I asked you at the start: *"Why do you want to go to college?"* One reason is to get a good job and succeed in a career. **To have that success, you have to do a lot in college to prepare yourself — a lot more than just get that degree.**

What are those things? By now, you can probably tick them off as fast as I can type them:

1. Gain knowledge in every one of your courses
2. Develop your learning skills so you can learn with efficiency later on in a career
3. Improve your communications skills
4. Use your classroom experiences to prepare for a job, any job, at any time of your life.

As you think about these important goals, think about this. You're obviously not going to love every college course, every professor, every assignment or test. No one can love everything in life, but *respecting most everything* is the mature thing to do. It's the college thing to do. So put a lot of space between yourself and students who still take the adolescent view, complaining *"I hate this,* or *I hate that,"* or *"This course is stupid. Why do I have to take it?"* or *"I'll never use this stuff. It's dumb."*

You're training your brain to think in different ways. What's more, you'll be surprised at what you use later on in life. Most adults will confirm this. Ask them.

College is the time to learn respect for what goes on around you. You'll carry that attitude with you throughout your life. So make *Broaden your view of life* #5 and add it to your list above.

COLLEGES AND DEGREE PROGRAMS: THINGS YOU SHOULD KNOW

Let's define some terms so we all understand what we're talking about. For example, do you know the difference between colleges and universities? And why it matters?

Under 4,000 students. These smaller institutions are often termed Liberal Arts Colleges. Naturally, they offer Liberal Arts majors: in the humanities, social sciences, and sciences. Some small colleges are also devoted to special areas like music, art, engineering, and business.

4,000+ students. University enrollments can range from 4,000 students to tens of thousands. Large schools consist of many colleges and degree programs and, therefore, offer many, many more majors to choose from. Almost all these colleges have Colleges of Liberal Arts (sometimes called "Arts & Sciences") just like the smaller schools. But students in these Liberal Arts Colleges can often take courses in other professional colleges to broaden their education: like Business, Journalism, Health Sciences and so forth.

And there's another distinction about large schools. They offer many more colleges and majors. Their professional colleges and majors point a student in a particular job/career direction. For example, consider the kind of majors offered by a College of Business Administration. Students can major in Management, Accounting, Economics, Marketing, Finance, etc. When graduates of a business college look for jobs, they look in specialized employment areas that match the names of their majors.

Engineering colleges provide another example. There's Mechanical Engineering, Biomedical Engineering, Electrical Engineering, Nuclear Engineering, Civil Engineering, and so forth. Just like degrees and majors in Business Administration, these different Engineering majors direct students to particular jobs, careers, and professions.

Professional colleges often have their own career advisers. Specific professional majors often require specific career advice.

DEGREE PROGRAMS AND MAJORS
Things you should know

Let's talk about how degree programs are designed.

Colleges and major departments often publish models for students' use. One way to learn about your degree program is to look at these models or examples. They can be handed out or posted on your college's website, or sometimes they are formally-printed manuals. Always look for these materials in your department or college. Collect as many as you can. They're usually well done and really helpful.

The largest number of students at universities usually major in the Liberal Arts college. Majors in those colleges — English, History, Sociology, and Sciences — are not considered professional because they're usually not job-directed.

So Liberal Arts graduates have a more challenging task identifying careers. That's why they have to start looking very early. Where should they start? All colleges and universities have advising offices that help students choose careers. They might be called Career Centers or Career Placement Offices.

Whatever they may be called, Liberal Arts students should find out where these offices are and visit them as soon as possible. There are a lot of careers and jobs out there for Liberal Arts graduates, but you have to research them with the guidance of a qualified adviser.

And don't forget to talk to your major department professors about where graduates with your major find jobs and careers. More and more major departments track their graduates, following their job-search successes.

A General Note: I've noticed that in the last few years some smaller colleges have renamed themselves, calling themselves "universities," for whatever reasons. They cannot provide the breadth of offerings of large universities.

SPECIALIZING WITHIN A PROFESSIONAL DEGREE

Let's return to what I said before about making decisions and add this thought. Even if you have selected a professional degree, say, Engineering, you still have to select a certain major from among Mechanical Engineering, Biomedical Engineering, Electrical Engineering, Nuclear Engineering, etc.

Make that decision as early as possible and feel confident about it. Your decision will keep you from wavering from one major to another. Wavering almost always means delaying graduation, and as we've agreed, you want to avoid that at all costs, because it does "cost" you too much.

> **The same cost advantage applies to figuring out early on that you've changed your mind. By that I mean that you discover that you'd rather NOT major in what you thought earlier.** For example, a student may decide to be a vet because he or she likes animals. But vet students also must have a love of the science that's involved. They sometimes don't realize that until they're in the program.

If that happens to you and your major, go looking for a new one before you have to lengthen your education. Note: Students often forget that **advisers can support students changing their minds as much as they help students stay on track. Go for advice.**

MORE SCHOOL AFTER COLLEGE? IT'S CALLED POST-GRADUATE EDUCATION.

What if you are considering extending your education beyond undergraduate college to attend graduate school or a post-graduate professional school? The latter refers to Dental School, Law School or a specialized Engineering program. Want an advanced degree in Tax Law? Architecture? Would you like to earn a master's degree or a PhD in graduate school?

These are decisions you have to make at least **by your second year of college.**

Post-graduate programs want good grades from the get-go. Here's a little bit of advice that pre-graduate and pre-professional school students don't realize until it's too late. If you plan on continuing your education after college, **the quality of your grade-point average must be excellent and apparent from your first semester onward.** Blow even one semester, and you'll likely have to cancel your post-graduate plans after college.

Do you hear an echo in the background? That's me reminding you once again that your first day of college is the first day of the rest of your life.

Here's a motto for you. Post this one on the inside of the door that you walk through to leave for classes:

<blockquote>
Your success in college will
determine your success in life.
</blockquote>

GOING TO MEDICAL SCHOOL?

You have to know if you want to pursue medicine by your **first semester freshman year.** That's because schools and colleges in various areas of medicine require certain science and sometimes math courses. You'll need them even to apply to Med School. Also, pre-med students are tested on their knowledge in those academic areas when they take qualifying tests.

And keep this in mind. Pre-med students can major in any academic area. It's true; most pre-med students major in the sciences (Biology, Chemistry, Physics). But those students have no better chance for admission than students who major in the non-sciences, no matter what anyone says.

To enter any "graduate" program requires that you pass a qualifying test. Those tests, along with your grade point average, determine your odds for admission. For example, if you want to go to dental school, you take the DAT, the Dental Admissions Test.

Let's say you want to become a lawyer. The test for admission to Law School is the LSAT, the Law School Admission Test. As a Pre-Law student in college, you don't have prerequisite courses to qualify for admission. You can major in any area you want from Psychology to Accounting to Music. Like all post-graduate degree programs, your chances for admission depend on your grade-point average, your quality as a learner, and your standardized test score.

MANY ADVISERS, MANY KINDS OF SPECIALISTS, EVEN CAREER HELP
Things you should know

You're independent. But getting advice from one-in-the-know can help. *Let's talk about independence some more. As I've said before, college is the time not only for making independent decisions, but also for developing good decision-making skills. You make good, solid, independent decisions when you think about them carefully, weighing options and estimating outcomes. However, when you're trying to reach really important decisions in your life, it's best to consult others who have more experience.*

YOUR ACADEMIC ADVISER

Now here's an important point: the best decisions are made after getting advice from experts. Your academic adviser is a person you can trust and who appreciates the importance of what you're trying to accomplish.

You might ask, *"But if I consult someone, is that really my independent decision?"* Yes it is, definitely. Asking for advice helps you sort things out. Your adviser may ask, *"Have you taken everything into account?"* Or, *"Think about it from this angle."* Or, *"This step looks like it will take you where you want to be long-term.'"*

Colleges and universities try hard to see that students are each assigned an adviser, if only to keep students on track: taking the right courses at the right time. That may seem so elementary that it's hardly worth mentioning. **But these elementary decisions are important, as well as deceptively tricky.** You'll make your life a whole lot easier by signing up for courses and taking them *in the right sequence.*

- Take, for example, that you're trying to decide about a major. The courses you select to take *and how you arrange them* can be crucial.
- If you change majors, how do you make sure you stay on track toward your degree?
- You may want to take a course during the summer at a college near your home. How do you make sure that course *will transfer? Meet the requirements of your degree?*

You want to get advice on such things. See your academic adviser. In short, academic advisers can answer a lot of questions that will make your decisions easier and better.

ADVISERS RELATED TO COURSES/MAJORS

When starting college, you're assigned a "Freshman Adviser" (sometimes called a "New Student Adviser" or "Pre-major Adviser.") These are all different names for the same person.

But if you have decided on a major as a freshman, you'd be assigned a "Major Adviser," a prof in the department in your major area of study.

Consult your adviser regularly. You may be *required* to do so. But even if you're not required, do it. Just as making sound, independent decisions is a skill you develop, so is getting in the habit of **seeking advice from knowledgeable people**. You want to make *informed decisions,* confident that you've weighed all factors involved in your decision. It's like confirming your decision with a tax accountant.

For example, these are the kind of crucial decisions that should not be made without consulting an adviser:

You may have decided on a major when you started college, but was it the right one? Talk it through with your adviser.

What if you decide to carry two majors? Sometimes it's possible. How do you fit your required courses for both into a four-year degree program?

ADVISERS FOR SPECIAL THINGS

You may have more than one adviser. For example, if you're thinking about continuing your education beyond college, you should consult an adviser who specializes in what's often called "pre-professional advising." Here are some examples of when you might need other advisers.

Foreign Study Advisers

More and more students are deciding to spend a semester or two studying in a foreign country. Your college or university may offer such programs. Or you might select a program from another college or university.

Obviously, this is one of those big decisions. Will studying abroad fit into your degree program without extending it? Will the courses you take abroad transfer to your home college and fulfill certain degree requirements? In short, how do you make a good decision about the right program for you? A Foreign Study Adviser is the person to consult.

Advisers for jobs, careers, professions

These decisions are big ones. And you should start getting advice about them very early in your college life. Don't be like far too many students who wait until two weeks before they're about to graduate and then say to themselves, *"Oh yeah, I guess I should think about getting a job!"*

Post-graduate, specialized advisers

You might be thinking about one of these careers or professions: a medical doctor or dentist or lawyer or veterinarian. These professions obviously require further study after college. But you need someone who can help you confirm that you're taking the required courses to go on into professional school to achieve your career goals.

Post-graduate professional schools require qualifying examinations. When do you take them? How do you prepare for them? What kind of scores do you need? What college grade-point overall? You need the knowledge/advice of specialized advisers.

Specialized Career Advisers

All colleges and universities have offices or departments that give students advice about identifying career options and how/when to talk with people visiting your campus who 1.) recruit students for certain jobs, and 2.) who can advise you on applying for those jobs.

These offices go by different names. There might even be more than one. The college in which your major resides might have a career adviser. But the larger Career Center would serve all students, especially students trying to identify areas of professional interest.

It's still your decision.

Whomever and whenever you ask for advice. However much or little that person contributes to your decision. IT'S STILL YOUR DECISION, YOURS ALONE.

You are always the one in control of your college life. But other, more experienced and knowledgeable, people can make you more confident about the decisions you make.

ADVISERS IN THE COUNSELING CENTER:
when you need help

W hen you're feeling overwhelmed, sad, a bundle of nerves, have any kind of problem, or don't know what to do about something, this is where you go. These people can help you. No matter if your struggle is personal or academic.

College students have so many adjustments to make that they frequently get overwhelmed. This feeling can show itself in many ways. A lot of students suffer from anxiety, depression, eating disorders, sleep deprivation, drugs, attempted suicides, binge drinking.

Given all these complications of life, as a student, you must be very aware of how you deal with the pressures of college. The best way is to get the advice of a counselor at a Counseling Center. Do it right away. Don't wait until things get bad.

Then there's the problem of sexual assaults and a "hook-up" culture of sexuality.

And know this: Most schools have counselors who specialize in issues of gender identity.

Anything you say to a counselor is absolutely confidential. While you may decide to tell your parents you're going for help, a counselor will never disclose the details of your discussions. You can reach these offices day or night.

KNOW WHERE TO GO FOR SERVICES ON CAMPUS. Get your money's worth!

W hether your campus is small, medium, or large, get to know it from one end to the other. Sure, you can see a campus map on your computer. But in-person observation is the best and most memorable way to learn.

Here are the places you should be familiar with. These are places you are likely to visit. Walk around campus, and recognize where they're located. Once you know where they are, you're more likely to use them.

1. **Adviser's Office.** Your academic adviser is one of the first — and also one of the most important — people you should get to know. Make sure you know how to find this person's office to get the individual academic advice you need.

2. **College Office.** A medium or large university consists of many colleges. You major department will reside there. It is a central office that can help you in many ways.

3. **Major Department.** Whatever your major, that major will have a central office. Like your college office, you'll probably have to go

81

there many times to make sure you're on the right track to complete your major coursework to graduate.

4. **Registrar's Office.** Do you have questions about registration? Your transcript? Your grades? This is the place to go.

5. **Bursar's Office.** This office handles money matters, from tuition to various other payments you have to make. It can give you some good general financial advice, too, to make sure you stay within your personal budget: for example, managing your credit card.

6. **Medical Center.** Have a bad case of the flu? A sprained ankle? Any other day-to-day health issues? Questions about your medications? This is the place to go. When you have serious health problems, this office will refer you to an affiliated hospital.

7. **Counseling Center.** The psychologists and counselors in this office help you with personal and emotional problems. If you're saying to yourself, *"I just don't feel like I have my feet on the ground. I worry a lot. I feel really depressed,"* you want to talk to a professional in this office. They really understand every kind of problem that a college student might experience. And, of course, this service is very personal, confidential, and free, as are all the services on this list.

8. **Student Affairs Office.** Go to this place to find out about extracurricular activities. From recreation to clubs to community service projects, this office handles all of these kinds of out-of-class activities that really make your college life feel complete.

9. **Police/Security Office.** As always, safety first is important. With any criminal act that you experience or witness, you should go to or call this office. Always follow the college's advice regarding your safety on campus, whether it comes from the Campus Police Office, Student Affairs, or the Counseling Center. Knowing what to do and what not to do as you move about your campus will ensure your safety.

10. **Tutoring Offices.** Many campuses have special offices to help students with certain academic problems, especially in writing and math. Besides your professors and academic adviser, these tutors can get you through some rough spots.

11. **Professors' Offices.** Know where each of your professors' office is. Visit them and introduce yourself. Tell them whether or not you have a background in their subject and why you're taking their course. Your visit can be short and casual.

   That way, when you have special questions about your courses, you'll already have met. It will be easier to approach this prof than seeing a stranger. College professors love to talk to students in and out of class. So know where their offices are and when they hold office hours. Syllabuses or course calendars contain this information.

A college campus is like a big ocean liner filled with people who want and need to do a lot of things. You're paying a lot for a great "trip," so make sure where everything is on this big vessel. Get your money's worth and take advantage of these services.

LIFE X 10: BIG CHANGES

I have often referred to college years as **Life times 10**. I want you to understand what that means. You're the one who will go through it.

During college, everything in your life changes so dramatically and rapidly that it's hard to keep up.

YOUR ACADEMIC LIFE

- ✓ You're making this big jump from high school to college in handling responsibility, self-reliance, and independence.

- ✓ You have to study so much more.

- ✓ You need a **Map** to stay on track. That's probably new, too.

- ✓ You have to manage learning course content in greater amounts and at faster rates every new semester.

- ✓ Your academic life multiplies in so many ways that you might feel like your life is approaching the speed of sound.

YOUR PERSONAL LIFE

This part of your life obviously doesn't just stop. In fact, it's also increasing speed.

- ✓ You're probably away from home or at least away from a high school schedule that kept you on-track during the school day. At first, not having that regimen seems like a great relief. You have freedom now.

✓ But from an academic point of view, you know that your new freedom and independence have to be balanced by keeping your work and your time under control.

✓ When your new lifestyle as a college student interferes with your studies, you know you're in trouble. So how do you handle this equally-changing balance in your personal life? See an adviser.

LIFE IN THE DORM

✓ You move into a residence hall or a dorm. As I said, they're like 24-hour shopping malls. So your living, sleeping, and eating environment is turned upside down.

✓ College students, especially the younger ones, don't like to sleep. More specifically, they don't like to sleep in normal ways – like in a bed from, let's say, 11:30 to 7:00 a.m. So you have to work around the noise. One of the worst things you can do is neglect sleep. (Buy a good set of drugstore earplugs.)

✓ Some college students like to avoid eating meals. I don't mean they avoid eating in general, but they prefer eating on the same schedule that they sleep – not very well. They're ordering out at all hours and eating fast-food rather than having the occasional vegetable. A caution about pizza and beer. Have your heard of the Freshmen 15? **That's how much weight freshmen girls gain.**

✓ Then there's the roommate. That experience spans everything from "great" to "he/she's driving me crazy!" Living in a dorm means living with someone who may have very different ideas about college and living in general. Getting along with that person is also another adjustment. A major one. You can manage that also.

There are ways for you to handle all of this, more later. Right now, we're just talking about the number of changes you're trying to adjust to. Don't forget this next item.

KEEP YOUR BODY IN SHAPE TO MAKE YOUR BRAIN WORK BETTER.

This means sleeping, exercising, and eating good food regularly. Yes, according to your **Map**. Too many students are determined to sleep less, sleep at the wrong times of day, eat more junk food, and never exercise. Bad news all around.

MAKING NEW FRIENDS

What about other people in your life? College is the time to form new friendships and enjoy other people with common interests and personalities. These are friends that you will bond with for life. It's true: College friendships are much more likely to endure than high school ones. That's because college relationships are so much more meaningful, deeper, and satisfying. You're turning into an adult with these people, and together, you're sharing the experience.

> On a very deeply personal level, building these friendships is just as important as learning in the classroom. In fact, I think the two things merge in many helpful ways.

With *real* friends — as opposed to party animals — you're much more likely to talk about your courses, personal things, and what you're going to do after college. These conversations create life-long friendships. More on that later.

College is the time for personal as well as intellectual growth. There's no reason why being a College Smart student should, in any way, cancel out having fun outside of classes and studying. Enjoying yourself makes your courses more enjoyable. You'll learn that one kind of growth enhances the other.

Making new friends gives you more confidence and helps you grow socially. You'll meet different kinds of people, maybe international students who show you a new view of the world.

Join clubs. Volunteer for community service with other students. **You'd be surprised how many college students don't know about the multitude of programs that colleges offer as extracurricular activities.**

CHOOSE FRIENDS WISELY.

✓ Find the right friends. Many students drink too much, experiment with drugs, or have zero respect for the other person in a relationship. In general, they're looking for wild times and do everything to ruin their lives.

✓ Stay away from it all. Avoid students who will lead you in harmful directions. Behavior like this will affect not only their college career, but their whole life. They think they're just having a good time or relieving stress — even though they're barely "working" at all. What they're really doing? Letting their lives go down the drain. Here's what happens.

- They may never recover to become students in the true sense.
- They certainly will never graduate on-time. Most likely, they'll never finish college, or they may spend lots of money in extra years in a "make-do" major that they don't really like.
- Their college transcript will be a disaster. Do they want to show it to a potential employer?

- They won't get their dream jobs.
- They'll never be able to go on in school, to graduate or professional school. What happens if they suddenly change their mind when they're older and want to?
- They won't be the constant learners that the workplace is looking for — and rewards.
- Who knows how their immature habits will spill over into their personal lives with regard to families?
- And they've squandered all that money in tuition, room, and board.

✓ **Know this:** You have crucial decisions to make, not only about study, but about lifestyles during college. These decisions can be challenging. But look out for yourself. Be careful and cautious. Be proud of your good decisions. Make the effort, and you can do it.

SEXUAL RELATIONSHIPS

When we talk about sexual relationships, they can often reach levels of emotional and very personal intensity. I'm talking about both short-term relationships and those longer-term relationships that may lead to life relationships.

Relationships take —

- a lot of maturity
- a great deal of common sense (often not that common in sexual relationships)
- the intelligence to keep it in perspective
- candor — openness, truthfulness, sincerity, honesty
- and, most of all, respect for the other person.

Respect is an important attribute for you to develop in college. In relationships with other people, it is essential.

At this point let me make some generalizations before continuing with your personal life in college.

So we agree that your daily academic and personal life in college requires big changes. And if we try to separate your life as a student from your life as a person, we should realize that each has its own challenges.

On the student side, you do all the things we talked about earlier to become a great College Smart student, to get the most out of the whole learning experience. When you get off the academic track, you consult your advisers, counselors, and professors.

On the personal development side, you're maturing in just as many ways, and perhaps entering into relationships that go along with all that. You also have people to turn to in this area of your life: the Counseling Center.

MATURE RELATIONSHIPS

Let's go back to close personal relationships. This isn't high school — with boy and girl friends.

Right off, get rid of those adolescent terms. They make personal relationships seem so superficial. College students are becoming young adults, and their relationships shouldn't be thought of this way.

In sexual relationships, *respect* and *respectful behavior* mean, that from the start, presume NOTHING about how the other person wants the relationship to unfold. The attitude of *"Oh, she really looks like this kind of person,"* or *"Oh, he really looks like that kind of guy,"* is judging based on inadequate information. Making such snap judgments is the worst kind of disrespect for the other.

As high school students, teens stumble around sexual activity as stupidly as their personal immaturity desires. However, now that you are in college, you have to be candid and upfront whenever you engage in even the briefest physical contact with another person.

One university (maybe more) adopted date cards. What's a date card? Well, on this card a student would indicate what activity he/she permitted in a new relationship. People laughed at the idea. I don't know if it's still being used anywhere. Imagine meeting a new person at a party. Before you dance, you whip out your date card and say, *"Oh, by the way, here's what you can and can't do."*

Funny? Having very personal, sexual restrictions printed on a card may seem silly or even absurd. **But I think the rationale behind the idea is very sound.** I would insist, if you don't have a card, you have to say, at some point, very specifically, what you will do and will not do.

You probably won't speak about such things when you first meet, but you'll know when the time comes for these things to be said. Things may change as a relationship develops, but those changes must still be expressed.

At this point you might want to say, *"Hey, Dr. Bob, can we get back to studies and college goals, etc.?"* **The truth is I've never left that subject. The very personal, sexual relations of college students naturally have a huge impact on their lives as learners.**

Nothing can throw a student off of a studying and learning track worse than a sexual relationship that is confusing, immature, erratic, or characterized by ridiculous teen-age absurdities about sex and close relationships.

Prevent these problems right from the beginning. Use candor and clarity. Without them, you can count on your life going into a tailspin, often with long recovery periods. I've seen it happen time and time again with students sitting in my office in a state of devastation.

SEXUAL ABUSE IS ON THE RISE.

Women are especially vulnerable.

I recommend that you go to the programs, seminars, and presentations about sexual relationships that all good colleges and universities offer their students, young and old. These events, in my opinion, are as important as those having to do with academics, like freshmen orientation and academic advising programs.

The truth is that colleges are, unfortunately, filled with catastrophe, violence, and even criminal behavior between and among students

within sexual relationships or even first-night relationships. College women are the greatest victims, as women usually are. Regarding sexuality, men can often be ignorant and aggressive to the point of being absurd and dangerous. Women are particularly vulnerable to that ignorance because, quite frankly, college students drink too much alcohol.

Being drunk or on drugs increases the danger. College men lose most of their rational control, and women become increasingly susceptible to male aggression. The repercussions of this mindless behavior extend from shocking and utter disrespect for another person to violence that may, and should, end in criminal charges.

IN THE AFTERMATH OF ASSAULT

Here is what you should know about the criminal nature of sexual assault among college students, both on and off campus. To my great regret, many colleges presume to make judgments about sexual offenses. They should no more being doing this than making judgments about a student who robs the bookstore.

If you are a college student who has been sexually assaulted, you should report it first to campus police and then to the local police.

To any victim I say that, as hard as these matters are to bring to light, do it to protect yourself from a reoccurrence. Get professional counseling help on campus, and get the justice you deserve. Not only are you protecting yourself, you may be protecting other prospective victims.

Students need the right counsel and advice in all these horrible situations. That's one of many reasons colleges have "counseling and health centers" to assist students in extremely personal circumstances. Trust these people. They know how to help you because, regrettably, they have become experts from helping many students with this experience.

Causes of sexual offense and assault are not limited to the realm of the perverts and perpetrators.

Alcohol, marijuana, and hard drugs trigger these acts in students, too.

The **sexual misconduct occurring among party-goers or others** at college gatherings on or off campus **can trigger anything** from unwanted sexual overtures to violence or abuse.

Take this advice to heart, too: It needs to be said, even at the risk of sounding like a parent talking to a young child. Here it is:

Stay away from people and situations that attract or promote unhealthy, immoral, abusive, dangerous, and criminal behavior. You know the difference. Many of you have already seen it in high school.

College campuses are not villages of perversions. Most students are sensible, level-headed, cautious, and, most of all, respectful. Like you! My advice? Stay away from the students who don't share your college values.

COLLEGE IS LIFE-CHANGING. Make good decisions. This isn't just "more school."

L ife is filled with questions that need answers — and decisions that have to be made. I hope you understand that by now.

Think of the decisions you've already had to make as you set your sights on college:

- taking the right courses to get ready for college
- preparing for standardized tests
- picking out colleges to apply to
- calculating cost and affordability for you and your family
- deciding which college to attend.

Those were all big decisions.

When you get to college, you want to make a great start, so you have even more decisions to make.

Here's your checklist.

✓ You have to get off on the right foot as a student who understands studying, learning, and mapping.

✓ You want to be sure you've chosen a major that's right for you.

✓ If you don't have a major, start talking to people who can help you make that decision ASAP!

All of these decisions will get you settled in college. You can spend more time on your studies right away and less on being bewildered and confused.

The decisions you made in high school launched you into college. The decisions you make in college launch you into your life and into the world. It's the BIG TIME!

FACING DECISIONS AVOIDS TROUBLE LATER ON… HOW IT UNFOLDS

This is a time of big, life-altering decisions. Far too many students delay these decisions because they're too BIG to face. Far too many students leave college not having a clue about what comes next. That won't be you.

In case you're interested, this is how the trouble unfolds.

#1 Leaning and majors. Because students don't face and make the big decisions about being a learner and finding a major, they fumble around academically, moving from one college to another, and getting poor grades. And after all that, they never graduate.

#2. No degree credential in searching for a job. Therefore, they cannot claim a college degree in looking for a job. And on the first pages of this book we said that getting **a good job and earning more money is overwhelming reason most students come to college.** What's wrong with this picture?

#3. In debt. Can you imagine anyone spending so much money on college and then end up with nothing? In fact, it's less than nothing. Why? See #4.

#4. What a prolonged degree implies, unless it's delayed for economic reasons. Think about it this way. A potential employer will be presented with a college record showing a 2.10 grade-point average, studded with course withdrawals, incompletes, and semesters at different colleges. Even if a student finally graduates, taking 5, 6, or 7 years, what kind of credential is that? What does that say about the candidate? Smart employers are beginning to draw conclusions.

RESEARCH ON HAPPINESS

Recall what I said early on about making a lot more money in your lifetime with a college degree vs. not having one? College offers more than money and job opportunities. **Researchers who study things like "how important education is in a person's life" have proven that —**

- A college degree will likely make a person healthier. College graduates have more awareness about the importance of healthy living throughout one's life.
- College graduates make better decisions about saving, spending, and investing money.
- Graduating even affects areas of your personal life – marriage, family, friendships, and relationships with colleagues.
- College affects qualities of character – honesty, generosity, dependability, determination, loyalty, and the list goes on.
- For sure, a college degree may not guarantee that you'll be a perfect human being, but in college, you'll learn what character is and how it applies to life.

A WARNING ABOUT THE LIST ABOVE.

These results are not guaranteed. It depends on the kind of college student you are. Are you engaged in your courses? Seriously invested in learning? (Notice the word, *invested*.) Developing and growing in maturity? Or are you the same person you were in high school — without focus and adolescent? All these things make a difference.

So don't ignore what college can do for you. You've been given an opportunity, a gift not given to everyone. Don't waste it.

THINGS YOU
NEED TO KNOW
AND TAKE
TO HEART.

That last section gives us a perfect transition to this section. Let's review again the things the many students don't realize college will do for them. When you know them, you're going to be way head of the herd.

1. College will help you gain knowledge to understand life and your purpose in it.
2. College will help you learn better. Even when you leave college, your life will be a constant learning effort, whether it's in your working life or in your personal life.
3. Your life will be filled with decisions. You'll use what you learned in college courses to make these decisions and pursue your goals as best you can.
4. By being in college, going to classes, managing your time well, studying regularly, and being responsible for your learning, you're practicing for being an excellent employee.
5. College will give you the opportunity to advance your communication skills. *Listen* attentively. *Talk* intelligently to your professors, advisers, friends, and classmates. Advance your *reading and writing* in all your courses. Know what you're doing? Developing the basic

skills — both in and out of your work life — that give you an easier way to manage and understand the challenges of life.

6. As a learner, a thinker, an analyst, a problem-solver, an idea person, you'll be in-demand when you are looking for a first job, and you'll go places in the workplace.

7. If you follow these concepts, your college experience will make your personal life better. You'll appreciate everything in life more fully. With that advantage, your chances of living a happier and longer life increase greatly.

College is the gift that gives you the edge. It leads you and develops you. Without college, you'd have to do this all on your own. It's very much harder.

There's an 8th point.

This point holds all the others together. It gives you control over the other seven. It makes them easier to use. It makes them an almost instinctive, automatic, and sensible.

Personal Maturity. Let's check out the meaning of maturity in a dictionary: *the state of being fully grown or developed*. Now that definition might refer to a financial investment or a tomato.

But when it applies to you, it becomes much more complicated. Our two examples are simple. As long as you have good financial advice, your investments should mature. As long as you water your tomato plants and give them plenty of sun and fertilizer, they'll grow.

I'm acting in both ways. I'm giving you advice. The advice acts as the conditions you will need to grow and mature.

Remember the young people who don't go to college, yet achieve happiness. Their maturity helps them. They are out in the world sooner than you will be. Don't use college to avoid maturing. Don't spend it as a "freedom" party and avoid your responsibility to mature.

TAKE THIS QUICK SELF-EXAMINATION. How far have you come since middle-school?

fter reading these pages, you should be wiser, seeing things more broadly than when you first opened this book.

Take this survey. It will help you examine your life from the time you started middle school until now. It will help you understand how you have changed (or not) mentally, intellectually, educationally. The survey is quick and easy. Let's go!

1. Over the past 6 or 7 years, have you learned how to control your life, from day-to-day, or does it control you?
2. Have you learned to be more independent over the years, or do you still need someone to supervise your life for you (like parents

and teachers)? Do they still get you where you need to be on time and with the stuff you need? Without that supervision, can you handle yourself?

3. Along the same lines of independence... Are you learning to make your own decisions, or are they made mostly by what your friends do? Do you always need their approval or have you learned to approve things for yourself? Can you be different?

4. Over the years, have your parents, teachers, advisers, and even employers and coaches trusted you to do the right thing? Or do you know or suspect that they worried that you won't. Why?

5. Have you realized this truth yet? The more independent you want to become and the freer you want your life to be, the more personal responsibilities you have to assume.

6. Go back to the definition of *mature*. As a person have you grown and developed in that sense? Do you understand that you're getting older and you have to think more about your life — where you want to go, who you want to be— so that you make **better decisions for YOURSELF? That's very different from just doing what you <u>want</u> to do.**

There are other questions you might ask yourself, but these are enough for you to understand what I'm getting at. We can condense all these questions into this one: **Over the years have you become more and more mature? Independent? Self-reliant? Responsible?**

When you're trying to evaluate yourself, it often helps to look around you. Take a look particularly at those people you know the best, your friends. Look at the people close to you, not necessarily in friendship, but those you see every day and bump into or cross paths with regularly — like classmates.

As you look at these other people in your life, how much are you like them? Let's get down and dirty, first. Do they spend more time having a good time than studying or planning out their lives? Are they always looking for new ways to increase their physical pleasures? Are drinking, drugs, and sex the things that are important from day-to-day?

As students, are they always behind, always on the edge of a deadline-cliff, always trying to find ways to study less, always blowing off classes, always trying to squeeze their way out of one tight academic spot or another? Do they take care of themselves, with regard to sleeping, eating, and getting exercise? Do they act in an immature way?

Anyway, you see where I'm going. You want to be the person, the student who can say, *"I'm not like them, and I won't become like them."* Take my word for this because I know it from years of experience: ***Students who are always doing the wrong things are always looking for others to do it with them.*** It makes them feel like their behavior is okay because *others are doing it, too.*

College is not the only time in a person's life to become mature; but it is the best time.

And if you don't become really mature in college, it may take years before you find the next opportunity.

Here's another motto for you: **"LIFE DOES NOT WAIT AROUND FOR PEOPLE TO BECOME MATURE!"** In fact, in its own cruel ways, life punishes people, especially young ones of college age, who are always behind the eight-ball when it comes to acting more mature.

So MATURITY summarizes all the others. When you can say *"I'm becoming more and more mature,"* you know you have all those other qualities you get with a good college education.

Go do great things!

Dr. Bob